Perspectives

Wildlife in the City

Why Should We Protect It?

Series Consultant: Linda Hoyt

Flying Start
to Literacy®

Contents

Introduction

Should we protect city animals?

Did you know that our cities are full of animals? As well as our pets, there are animals in parks, roaming the streets after dark and building nests in trees.

These animals are wild animals. Unlike our pets, they find their own food, shelter and water. They live without help from people.

How do we live with them? Are they dangerous?

Take a city safari

Written by Megan Hansen

The number of different wild animals that live in your neighbourhood might surprise you!

If you went on a city safari, what do you think you may find?

1 Use your binoculars to scan the rooftops, power lines and treetops around you. Are possums scurrying past? Do hawks circle overhead?

2 Look between cracks in footpaths and blades of grass. How many ants, earthworms or (eek!) cockroaches can you find?

3 Search for signs of wildlife: bird droppings on the footpath or tunnels dug in park flowerbeds. Can you tell what animal may have left these signs?

4 Even though you're in the city, remember the motto: *Take only pictures, leave only footprints.* Keep your eyes open and you may make some amazing discoveries!

Speak out!

Read what these students think about wild animals in cities.

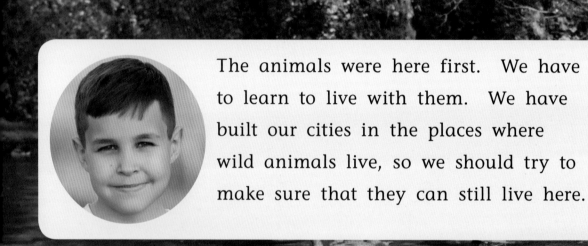

The animals were here first. We have to learn to live with them. We have built our cities in the places where wild animals live, so we should try to make sure that they can still live here.

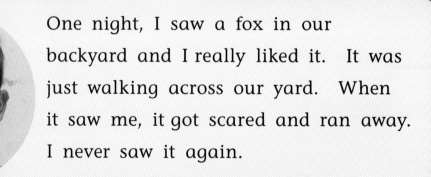

One night, I saw a fox in our backyard and I really liked it. It was just walking across our yard. When it saw me, it got scared and ran away. I never saw it again.

One night, my dad was annoyed with the huge possum that was eating the flower buds on his favourite tree. He wanted to scare the possum to make it go away, so he tried to shake the branch of the tree with a long stick. But the night was wet and dark, and the stick fell on my dad and cut him. He had to go to the hospital. He really doesn't like the possums now!

We used to have chickens, but one night a fox came into our yard and stole a chicken. We don't keep chickens anymore because we're scared the fox will come back.

Urban foxes

You might not know this, but foxes have made themselves at home in our towns and cities. Our cities are full of food for them — mice, birds, small animals or your leftover pizza! Some people love foxes; others think they are a problem.

Read what people say about foxes. What do you say?

People who like foxes say:

- Foxes help control pests. They eat rats and pigeons.
- Foxes are noisy, but so are cats and dogs. What's the difference?
- Foxes don't hunt cats and dogs.

People who don't like foxes say:

- Foxes are noisy when they fight with each other.
- Foxes eat chickens and rabbits that people keep in their gardens.
- Foxes spread some diseases through their waste.

Too many bats!

Did you know that thousands of bats live in the trees in our cities? Most of the time you wouldn't notice these nocturnal animals. But when too many bats move to the one place, this can cause big problems.

Read about the dilemma that people faced when the bat population exploded in Melbourne's Royal Botanic Gardens.

Why did bats come to the gardens?

The grey-headed flying fox is a type of native Australian bat. These bats have lost much of their natural habitat because people have cleared more and more bushland to make way for homes, roads and buildings.

The bats have had to find new homes, and many now live in trees in city parks and gardens.

By 2001, there were about 30,000 bats living in the Royal Botanic Gardens, right in the centre of Melbourne.

What problems did they cause?

So many bats living together in the one city park caused some big problems.

The bats were noisy! And, they were smelly! The smell and noise made things very unpleasant for people to enjoy the park.

Also, the bats were damaging the rare and important trees they were living in. So it was decided that the bats had to be moved.

How was the problem fixed?

Everyone knew the bats had to go, but no one could work out how! Then one group came up with a plan.

Early one morning, a group of volunteers and park workers gathered in the park. When the signal was given, they all began making the loudest noise possible – they slammed dustbin lids together and blasted music from portable stereos.

The bats were startled. Thousands of them screeched as they flew out of the trees and into the sky. The bats flew to a much bigger natural bushland setting. It was here that the bats settled and have stayed ever since.

How to write about your opinion

State your opinion

Think about the main question in the introduction on page 4 of this book. What is your opinion?

Research

Look for other information that you need to back up your opinion.

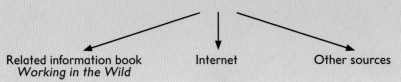

Related information book
Working in the Wild   Internet   Other sources

Make a plan

Introduction

How will you "hook" the reader to get them interested?

Write a sentence that makes your opinion clear.

List reasons to support your opinion.

Support your reason
with examples.   Support your reason
with examples.   Support your reason
with examples.

Conclusion

Write a sentence that makes your opinion clear. Leave your reader with a strong message.

Publish

Publish your writing.

Include some graphics or visual images.